Summer afternoon—summer afternoon; to me those have always been the two most beautiful words in the English language.

Henry James (1843–1916)
American novelist

Long live the sun which gives us such color.

Paul Cézanne (1839–1906)
French painter

I expand and
live in the warm day like
corn and melons.

Ralph Waldo Emerson (1803–1882)
American essayist and poet

Beach Pails

BEACHPAILS

Classic Toys of the Surf and Sand

by Carole and Richard Smyth

RUNNING PRESS
PHILADELPHIA • LONDON

© 2002 by Running Press
Photographs © 2002 by Michael Weiss
All rights reserved under the Pan-American and
International Copyright Conventions
Printed in China

9 8 7 6 5 4 3 2 1
Digit on the right indicates the number of this printing

Library of Congress Cataloging-in-Publication Number 2001094107

ISBN 0-7624-1203-8

Cover and interior photographs by Michael Weiss
Cover and interior design by Frances J. Soo Ping Chow
Edited by Melissa Wagner
Typography: Itc Berkeley and Univers

This book may be ordered by mail from the publisher.
Please include $2.50 for postage and handling.
But try your bookstore first!

Running Press Book Publishers
125 South Twenty-second Street
Philadelphia, Pennsylvania 19103-4399

Visit us on the web!
www.runningpress.com

AT THE SEA-SIDE

When I was down beside the sea

A wooden spade they gave to me

To dig the sandy shore.

My holes were empty like a cup.

In every hole the sea came up,

Till it could come no more.

from *A Child's Garden of Verses* by Robert Louis Stevenson (1850–1894)
Scottish novelist, poet, and essayist

TABLE OF CONTENTS

INTRODUCTION:
Simple Pleasures and Happy Memories

JUST LOOK AT A VINTAGE tin beach pail and the happy memories of childhood summers come flooding back: vacations on the coast or at the lake shore, digging for buried treasure—maybe even building sandcastles or burying a willing dad in the sand. Before Disney World, Caribbean Cruises, Las Vegas, or touring in an RV or an SUV, the dream vacation for most families was to spend a week at a shore resort. Those who lived close to the coast considered themselves especially blessed, for they could visit the beach on weekends throughout the summer season.

For children, the highlight of those simple times was the fun of splashing around in the shallows, braving the waves, hunting for crabs, collecting shells, and simply playing in the sand. Ice cream, hot dogs, pony rides, and miniature golf were not then the seaside attraction that they are today. Once, the best time for many kids was building a sandcastle, and all that was needed was a beach pail, a spade, and maybe a few molds for decorating the sand.

A memorable part of the ritual was going off in late spring to the local five and dime, Woolworth's, or local corner variety store, which was inevitably stacked with a new crop of sand pails and other beach toys, set out just to entice youngsters. Part of the fun was selecting a pail from the vast array of wonderful, brightly colored scenes—traveling in outer space, undersea adventures, the circus acts, pirate ships, nursery rhymes, and cartoon characters. The possibilities seemed endless with a new sand pail, beach tools, and summer about to begin. Back then, mothers who accompanied children on these excursions were able to stock up for the season for less than a dollar or two.

Once at the glorious beach, the perfect site for the castle always made itself apparent right away. It had to be close to the water so that the sand was moist enough to hold its shape, but back far enough that the incoming tide wouldn't wash it away before it was done. (The spot was often conveniently within view of a watchful circle of adults, which offered the castle some protection from being trampled by the big kids throwing footballs.)

For a littler kid, filling the bucket required a seemingly endless series of shovels full of sand. Even with a good-size spade, it was an enormous task for little hands. Then, after stamping down the sand to make sure it was solid, it was time to turn it over and tap the upside-down bucket ever so gently with a spade. You'd find yourself holding your breath or sticking your tongue out of the corner of your mouth as you made the final, tricky maneuver. If you were lucky, lifting the bucket revealed a perfect turret. But usually, this perfection didn't last long—any number of things could cause it to come smashing down into a pile of sand. Thankfully it was often just at this moment that a father would rush over, revealing himself once again to be the best sandcastle builder ever!

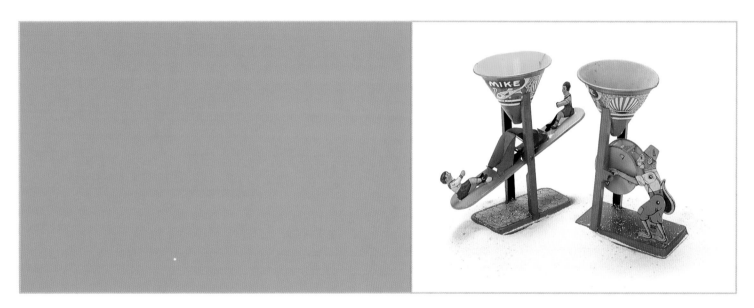

The long process of filling in the sand castle moat meant repeated treks to the water using both hands to carry the now-heavy pail back to the castle—and usually a rest was needed halfway. Running back to the castle only meant more trips, since by the time you got there the pail would some-how be only half full.

The trusty pail—its handle an extension of your hand on lazy summer afternoons—was always at the ready for the moment when you spotted the prettiest, most colorful seashells to adorn your castle. The best shells seemed often to require dashes into the water in between the waves.

Transporting your haul back to the castle, maybe you'd stop at your parents' blanket to present the treasure trove in the bucket for their approval. Often these gems were too valuable to be left behind at the end of the day. They'd be safely packed into the pails and brought home and saved, along with other childhood treasures.

One of the many things that made beach pails unique among toys is their universality. They were equally appealing to girls and boys, and were affordable to almost anyone. You didn't even have to live by the sea or lake to enjoy them—all you needed was a sandbox (or even a source of mud) and your imagination. Today, in our fast-paced, computer-animated

world, there is nostalgia for these simple childhood icons, which have been remembered fondly by adults for close to a hundred years. For generations, starting in the late 1800s, children looked forward at the beginning of each summer to a new bucket and spade—a signal of the months of the carefree fun ahead.

This started to change in the mid-1960s, when the far less romantic plastic pails became more popular. True, it didn't rust if you left it lying around in water; it didn't break if you trod on it; it didn't have any sharp metal edges; it floated. But there was no where near the quality and detail in the graphics. Half the fun was gone. By the mid-1970s, parents bought only the safe, durable, and (above all) dull plastic pails. Most tin pails were left to rust, but some have survived as reminders of happy, simpler days, when fifty cents meant not only a beach pail and a spade but a cream soda to boot!

There were a number of lithographed tin toys produced over the years, but sand pails were some of the simplest to make. The large outside surface provided a perfect canvas for illustrations, and these same graphics are what lend sand pails their special value among some of the most serious collectors of antiques.

It was the Victorians who really brought the seaside vacation into mainstream life, and along with this lifestyle came early sand toys. A surprising number of these first examples are available. Tracing the development of sand pails—from the hand painting of the Victorians, through the wonder years of great lithography, to the tin pails' gradual fall out of vogue—is a fascinating story.

Summer afternoon—summer afternoon; to me those have always been the two most beautiful words in the English language.

Henry James (1843–1916)
American novelist

These delightful pails show children at play, the all-time favorite theme for pails.
The smaller of the two doubled as a candy container.

This pail, made by T. Conn of Brooklyn, serves as a reminder that pails were also popular at inland lakes and swimming holes.

Summer is the time

when one sheds one's tensions

with one's clothes, and

the right kind of day is jeweled balm

for the battered spirit.

A few of those days and you can

become drunk with the belief that

all's right with the world.

Ada Louise Huxtable
American critic and editor

THE WATER THREW OFF a white light on the white sidewalk by the shops on the Riviera. . . . She had a straw bag and blue espadrilles. The children were eating dishes of ice cream with wafers pointing up. They were playing tag with the waves.

From *Evening* by Susan Minot
American author

All dressed up for a busy day by the sea—this happy pail was created by Whittaker Glessner Company, one of the smaller and rarer manufacturers.

C stands for collectible: this very popular design by the United States Metal Toy Manufacturing Company was perhaps a gentle reminder that the first day of school was not so far away.

I bought a dress,
a romantic dress, a purely summer party dress:
white, splashed with large pink dots,
a floppy full skirt and bared shoulders. A dress
for a summer tan, a summer dance.

Alice Adams (1927–1999)
American author

Long live the sun which gives us such color.

Paul Cézanne (1839–1906)
French painter

This pail is typical of the small, mustard-colored pails made by Kirchof,
a company that is best known for manufacturing party noisemakers.

In post-World War II Europe, sand pails were often made from metal scraps using pre-war printing techniques and simple designs.

Sunburn is very becoming—

but only when it is even—one must be careful

not to look like a mixed grill.

from *The Lido Beach* by Noël Coward (1899–1973)
British dramatist

THE DAY OF THE SUN is like the day of a king. It is a promenade in the morning, a sitting on the throne at noon, a pageant in the evening.

Wallace Stevens (1879–1955)
American poet

All the best resorts had a Punch and Judy puppet show, and some even had a circus complete with clowns, as seen on the pail by T. Bros (bottom right).

Friendly frogs hop around this pail of unknown origin.

Dandelion wine.

The words were summer on the tongue.

Ray Bradbury
American author

I expand and
live in the warm day like
corn and melons.

Ralph Waldo Emerson (1803–1882)
American essayist and poet

About to get a rude awakening, this happy dad is typical of T. Cohn's
playful depictions of farm animals.

Marked "Montevideo," this unusual but striking design may have Italian origins.

For him in vain

the envious seasons roll

Who bears eternal summer

in his soul.

from "The Old Prayer" by Oliver Wendell Holmes (1809–1894)
American physician, poet, and humorist

June is just waiting,

July is the beginning of the end.

Where is an unperturbed,

lasting summer?

Nowhere else but in our thoughts

during the winter.

Kersti Bergroth (1886–1975)
Finnish writer

The lid makes this pail exceptional. Pails often start life as candy containers, usually with lollipops in small ones and saltwater taffy in the larger sizes. This one may have English origins, since Lyons teahouses were the Starbucks of the 1920–60s.

This rare find is a wonderful example of a pail from the early 1900s.
The seaside scene is absolutely charming, but the remembrance of the Maine
on the base makes this pail by Sentenne and Green a blockbuster.

August creates as she slumbers,

replete and satisfied.

from *The Twelve Seasons* by Joseph Wood Krutch (1893–1970)
American writer

WHAT IS SO RARE as a day in June?

Then, if ever, come perfect days.

from "The Vision of Sir Launfal" by James Russell Lowell (1819–1891)
American poet and editor

Cars, planes, and trains are often hints to the age of a pail.
Children's clothes also provide clues.

The pail on the right is typical of those produced near the turn of the century, with its simple, silhouetted graphics and its unpainted interior. Though the pail above sports similarly uncomplicated graphics and printing techniques, the painted interior provides a clue that it was produced later.

Nearly every season I note what I call

the bridal day of summer—a white, lucid, shining day,

with a delicate veil of mist softening all outlines.

John Burroughs (1837-1929)
American naturalist

Any parent who has ever found a rusted toy automobile buried in the grass or a bent sand bucket on the beach knows that objects like these can be among the powerful things in the world. They can summon up in an instant, in colors stronger than life, the whole of childhood at its happiest—the disproportionate affection lavished on some strange possession, the concentrated self-forgetfulness of play, the elusive expressions of surprise or elation that pass so transparently over youthful features.

from *Sports Illustrated*
December 1960

This popular sand toy by J. Chein fascinated children
as the falling sand spun the spoon-paddled wheels.

Made in England, this early Happynak pail depicts a frog, mouse, owl, and lamb marching band.

When I was a little kid,

of course,

I was brown all summer.

That's because I was free as a bird—

nothing to do but catch bugs

all day. . . .

Roy Blount, Jr.
American humorist, author, and performer

W

hat we remember from childhood we remember forever—permanent ghosts, stamped, imprinted, eternally seen.

Cynthia Ozick
American author

The Elsie Dairy Pail is atypical of Ohio Art designs and was probably made under contract. It is now collectible as a character pail.

The History
of Sand Toys

NOWADAYS, an Internet search for "sand toys" is likely to direct you towards a website about high-powered beach buggies or some such fast-paced activity. Yet there are many of us for whom the mention of sand toys conjures up images of buckets, spades, sifters, sprinkling cans, and molds strewn across a golden beach on a sparkling summer day. There are those of us that still remember those wonderful Charles Atlas advertisements that claimed to turn lesser beings into muscle-bound men. The history of the tin sand pail traces back more than one hundred years and reaches beyond the production of the toy itself. To tell it fully it must also include the story of leisure, vacationing, and the American seaside resort as the country moved through periods of great change, including war, the Depression, industrialization, prosperity, and commercialization.

Early Sand Toys

In the early years of the Victorian era, sand toys meant something quite different from what we think of today. At that time they were designed for play indoors. Typically, a wooden or cardboard box with a glass front enclosed a cardboard scene of people or animals. The scene was brought to life by a simple mechanism powered by sand, which when poured into a chute turned a paddle wheel and caused rods and levers to animate the figures.

These Victorian sand toys were imported from Europe—mainly Germany, France, and England. By around 1825, American toy manufacturers, seeing the popularity of the imports, began fabricating their own versions. Today these are extremely rare, as most have presumably worn out over the years from use by eager young hands. Later, American artisans developed other types of sand toys that were free-standing. These also made use of sand that was poured down a chute, either to fill a railroad car or power a figure, wheel, or paddle. The classic mechanical sand toy was the "Sandy Andy," produced by the Sand Toy Company of Pittsburgh. They patented and made the toy starting in 1909, and continued to make it with various modifications even when they were later bought by the Wolverine Supply and Manufacturing Company.

Sand Toy Pioneers

Beach pails, as we know them today, did not exist before the Victorians popularized the seaside vacation in the second half of the 1800s. It wasn't until the 1870s that toy makers began to realize the potential for this new market and devel-

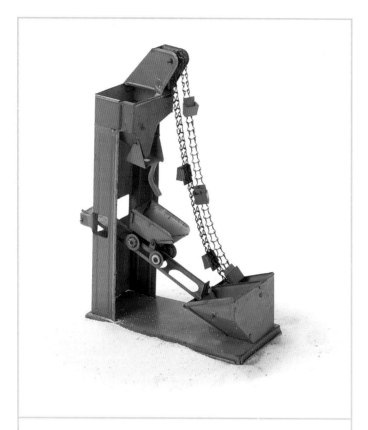

48 Beach Pails

oped a range of toys for child's play during those precious days at the shore. Suddenly the small wooden buckets and shovels children used to help their parents in the garden or with other chores around the home were transformed into highly desirable playthings when given a coat of brightly colored paint.

Other attempts to make marketable toys out of around-the-house tools were not as successful. For example, a water pump, first made as a replica of the farm yard pump, did not quite catch on. Even the watering (or sprinkling) can—while very helpful in building castles—has not evolved as the mainstay that the beach pail became.

The use of cookie-cutters and molds for baking in the kitchen was particularly inspiring to Jesse Crandall, a member of the family that owned the Crandall Toy Manufacturing company, which produced toys in America for nearly a century starting in about 1830. Benjamin Potter Crandall had begun his business in Westerly, Rhode Island, making a few toys and the first baby carriages manufactured in America. Benjamin

moved his family and business to New York in 1841 and his sons, including Jesse (born 1833) joined him. The whole family was prolific with patented ideas, and Jesse developed his first invention at the tender age of eleven.

By around 1875, Jesse was far more interested in making toys than anything else. The Civil War (1861–65) took its toll on the Crandall family business, since they could not collect on unpaid bills from the Southern states. Jesse took the opportunity to go to Ohio, where he taught the art of toy making to prisoners. When he returned to New York, the family had restarted the business of manufacturing carriages, and Jesse went out on his own, setting up a toy business in Brooklyn.

Crandall's most important patent in the history of beach toys is the "Sandometer," dating from 1879. He had been working on a child's rowing machine when he thought of this idea for a sand mold kit, which included a box of sand and a number of molds in different shapes. The more expensive version (six dollars, versus thirty cents for the basic kit) even included a table to build on. This idea offered an alternative to kids who were using their mother's flour and kitchen utensils, providing them with a set of tools of their very own. The advertisements claimed that the kit was "the Coney Island beach brought to your home." Crandall's sand molds were such a great success that the editor of *The Brooklyn Eagle* called him "The Child's Benefactor." He died in his nineties, after a long and productive life—and even a stint as Santa Claus in the A. Batterman and Co. store in New York City, which seems fitting for one who did so much for children.

THE EVENTS OF CHILDHOOD do not pass but repeat themselves like seasons of the year.

Eleanor Farjeon (1881–1965)
British writer, poet, and playwrite

Two sizes and two views of the same design that was frequently used by J. Chein under contract to Stover Candies Inc. of Hershey, Pennsylvania.

Although umarked, this pail is typical of the German imports that inspired the early work of the Ohio Art Company.

How dear to this heart are the scenes
of my childhood,

When fond recollection presents them to view.

from "The Old Oaken Bucket" by Samuel Woodworth (1784–1842)
American author and poet

HOW STRANGE are the tricks of memory, which, often hazy as a dream about the most important events of a man's life, religiously preserve the merest trifles.

from *Sind Revisited* by Sir Richard Francis Burton (1821–1890)
English writer and adventurer

Pails marked SEASIDE evoke early memories and
are always popular with collectors. Dated 1920 and manufactured
by Homework MFG, USA, seesaw pails (left) provide great clues
when estimating the age of similar examples.

From Wood to Tin

Several of the early American toy makers who had access to the new developments coming out of Europe played a role in transforming the more utilitarian wooden farm bucket into a recreational tin beach pail. Several small businesses in Massachusetts, including W. L. Woodcock, G. S. Greenwood, and the Heywood Brothers, were making wooden pails in the mid-1800s. Around that time, William Tower of Hingham, Massachusetts, a carpenter, was making wooden toys in his spare time, and learned of other tradesmen doing the same thing. An owner of an ax factory was creating toy tools, another craftsman made doll house furniture, and a third artisan was making toy pails, tubs, swings, ten pins, and furniture. It was Tower's idea that together they could form a cooperative guild. In time, this would come to be known as the Tower Guild, and it continued to produce toys until around 1915.

By the 1830s and 1840s, wood was no longer the preferred material for toys, as other materials—especially tin plate—became more plentiful. An abundance of tin factories emerged in the northeastern United States, ranging from large factories to small tin shops. Toy makers in Berlin and New Britain, Connecticut, did use tin starting in about 1815, and some of these workers also crafted their wares in southern states during the winter months.

Crafting Early Pails

The earliest tin toys were made from twelve-by-fourteen-inch sheets of tin plate, imported from Wales. Because of the sheets' small size, a pail could be only as big as five inches in diameter if it were made from a single sheet. The parts were then soldered together and the toy was finished in bright colors. Some pails were also decorated with lettered stencils and other detailing that was done by hand.

In the 1840s tinsmiths in Meriden, Connecticut, began using tin to make toys. This proved to be so popular that the industry grew rapidly, and factories specializing in tin toys cropped up not only in Connecticut but in New York and Philadelphia as well. According to an advertisement in the Maine Business Directory of 1856, Bradford Kingman of Boston was manufacturing toy pails, carriages, wagons, sleds, and rocking horses.

By the late 1800s, the technology of tin plate had developed, and American manufacturers were making large, thinner sheets and no longer had to rely on imports. One early American tin pail maker was George W. Brown, born in 1830 in Bolton, Connecticut. Along with Chauncy Goodrich, he founded George W. Brown and Company Toy Makers in 1856. Another pioneering partnership was that of Hull and Stafford (later Hull and Wright). Located in Clinton, Connecticut, a town famous for its tin toys, they made every sort of brightly painted tin toy imaginable from about 1870 to 1890.

One toy manufacturer in particular was successful at making the transition from wood to tin. Morton Converse was the first big-business beach pail manufacturer to mass-produce beach pails. He started production in 1878 at Winchendon, Massachusetts, first making wooden toys (he is well-known for his Noah's Arks, hobby horses, and rocking horses). At one time Winchendon was home to such a proliferation of toy manufacturers that it was known as "Toy Town, U.S.A." By 1890, Converse's company was considered the largest wooden toy manufacturer in the world. After several years with a partner, from 1878 to 1883, when the company was known as Mason & Converse, he again took sole control of the business. In 1890 he invested in the New England Lock & Hinge Company, so that he would have metal parts for his wooden toys. Shortly afterward he started manufacturing tin shovels and pails and was soon making well over a million of these a year. A company slogan was, "If it's made out of tin, we make it." The company continued to grow until 1929, by which time Converse had over three hundred workers. Tragically, within five years it would fall victim to the Great Depression and go out of business.

Cony Island: The Classic Seaside Resort

For much of the nineteenth century in America, seaside adventures had been limited to the wealthy, even for beaches that were close to cities. During the final decade of the nineteenth century, however, the economy was booming. The main mode of transportation was still horse-drawn carriages, but improved roads to the shore meant that trips were much more comfortable and therefore more popular.

Coney Island's Manhattan Beach Hotel, built in 1887, was typical of the era. Some seven hundred feet in length, this rambling wooden structure was set back from the sea, with lush, green lawns and flowering borders of geraniums and lobelias. The best rooms had porches facing the sea, and guests spent their days promenading along the hotel's walks or watching the children play on the beach.

This was a time when the sea was still largely for admiring and less for swimming. Saltwater bathing was all the rage, so long as it was done in the privacy of a bathhouse. The Manhattan Bathing Pavilion sported 2,350 individual bathhouses, plus an additional three hundred fifty larger rooms for groups of six. The bathers rented their blue flannel bathing suits from the bathhouse, which laundered two thousand suits an hour! Also at this time, in 1884, thrill seekers could ride Mr. Thompson's Switchback Railroad, the world's first roller coaster.

Coney Island afternoons were spent gambling at one of the three racetracks, at least until around 1908 when the newspaper mogul William Randolph Hurst led the fight to make track betting illegal. In the evenings, parents would enjoy a formal dinner—little neck clams, baked bluefish, roast lamb with all the trimmings, maybe a meringue glacé for dessert. Then it was off to the ballroom to hear John Philip Sousa lead the band in his latest inspirational marches. For the ladies, the night came to a close after Henry Pain's fireworks display of rockets, bombs, and giant catherine wheels, celebrating occasions like the defeat of the Spanish Fleet at Manila. Some men would then head off to bars or other establishments that offered gambling or even showgirls, such as The Gut in West Brighton, The Bowery off Surf Avenue, or the Silver Dollar Saloon.

Another major influence on the growth of the American tin toy industry was Leo Schlesinger, Inc. Founded in 1875 in New York, this company manufactured tin toys, including millions of sand pails that sold at ten cents each. Schlesinger went on to become one of the most important men of the toy industry, particularly in the years before and during World War I. Thanks to the efforts of Schlesinger's Association of Toy Manufacturers, which he formed in 1916 with sixty-eight other toy companies, these manufacturers were allowed to continue with toy production while they also made products for the war effort.

By the 1870s, American factories were producing in excess of forty million tin toys a year and the demand was growing each year. A shift was taking place in American culture, and by the 1890s a trip to the shore had become a popular pastime.

Methods of Design

One of the elements that made the first tin pails unique is their colorful design. The earliest pails were very simple in this respect and were decorated by a technique known as Japanning. This consisted of applying several layers of paint followed by a coat of lacquer. If a second color was used, it was applied by hand in bands as the pail was rotated on a turntable. As the market for these pails grew, the range of decorations grew more complex. After the initial coat of paint, lettering or other simple designs were added with a rubber stamp, stencil, or by hand.

Dyeing was a second, cheaper method of decoration, imported from France. A varnish-and-paint mixture was burned on and then the pails were baked, creating a very thin, hard, translucent finish which was extremely attractive.

Embossing was another common technique, used to accentuate a design or lettering. This involved stamping a pattern or decoration into a sheet of tin before it was made into a pail, so that certain parts of the surface were raised up. It was then very easy to paint the raised portions a second color, using either a paint pad or a roller.

The turn of the century was time of many technological changes, including the introduction of simple one- or two-color lithography. While some lithographed pails had been made in the 1890s, this method became more standard in the following decade. The process, which eventually replaced Japanning and stenciling, is best explained by the English term "tin printing," as it is, in effect, printing on metal with color. Minute detail that was impractical with the other processes now became possible, and the finish was extremely smooth. Various colors and details were printed on flat sheets of metal by a lithographic press, and the toys were then formed from these with presses and dies.

T. Bros produced several patriotic pails, which have always been popular,
but are especially relevant during times of national strife.

Memory is not so brilliant as hope,

but it is more beautiful, and a thousand times as true.

from *Prenticeana* by George Dennison Prentice (1802–1870)
American editor and writer

In memory

everything seems to be set to music.

from *The Glass Menagerie* by Tenessee Williams (1911–1983)
American playwrite, poet, and writer

Making music with a sand pail? This unusual and intriguing pail, although unmarked,
is reminiscent of others made by AMSCO of Elizabeth, New Jersey.

Just one of a whimsical series of animal scenes produced by
J. Chein & Co. during their golden years.

To be able to enjoy one's past life is to live twice.

from *Epigrams* by Martial (38–103 A.D.)
Roman poet

Every time we walk along a beach

some ancient urge disturbs us so that we find ourselves

shedding shoes and garments or scavenging among seaweed and

whitened timbers like the homesick refugees of a long war.

from *The Star Thrower* by Loren Eiseley (1907–1977)
American author, poet, and anthropologist

It's easy to see why Ohio Art hired Elaine Ends Hileman
to depict many aspects of children at play. This one is numbered 179.

Retailing in the Golden Age of Toys

At the same time the seaside was being discovered as a destination, major changes were taking place in the marketplace in terms of retailing. Department stores started to focus on toys in new and enthusiastic ways. The traveling peddler was being replaced by smaller stores like the five and dime, which were springing up all over. Mail-order catalogues were providing an unprecedented number of goods to many rural communities. The toy business was one of the industries that benefited greatly from this shift.

New York City's famous F. A.O. Schwarz Toy Store had been founded in 1870 by Frederick Schwarz, who had started out in the toy retailing business at Schwerdtmann's in Baltimore. His three brothers sold toys as well: Henry in Baltimore, Richard in Boston, and Gustav in Philadelphia.

In 1837 the aptly named George Doll opened a toy shop, in later years called The Temple of Fancy, in what is today the Northern Liberties section of Philadelphia. The store remained there for many years. George's brother John joined the venture and together their retail and import business flourished. In 1879,

John was bought out by his son, who, the following year, at age 33, founded the now-famous John Wanamaker Department Store. He remained their toy buyer for many years, traveling the world to purchase toys directly from manufacturers. He became known in trade journals as "the Dean of Toy Buyers."

R. H. Macy & Co., founded in 1857, recognized the popularity of toys by creating a year-round toy section in their stores, with special displays for Christmas. By 1874 their advertisements confidently claimed to have the largest variety of toys of any establishment, and by the 1880s their toy catalog had well over one hundred pages. Still, Gimbal's and Bloomingdale's were soon providing intense competition.

This was also the heyday of the mail-order houses, with Aaron Montgomery Ward starting out in 1872. The company stocked some toys by 1877 and had a huge selection by 1885. Sears Roebuck & Co., who opened in 1888 selling watches, were stocking a modest selection of toys by the turn of the century. Mail-order houses offered mainly mechanical sand toys, possibly since beach pails retailed for so little (between five and ten cents each).

While department stores and catalog companies flourished at selling more expensive toys, a revolution in retailing was responsible for bringing tin beach pails to the masses: the five and dime stores. By the 1890s there were thousands of these stores throughout the country. The most successful was F. W. Woolworth & Co., established early in 1879 in Utica, New York. This chain became the major seller of inexpensive tin toys, together with drug stores located in the seaside resort towns.

Design Motifs

A number of milestones in American history have resulted in related motifs found on tin beach pails. The Spanish American War (1898) brought a surge of patriotism that resulted in sand pails decorated with flags, eagles, and patriotic sayings, that represent some of the finest work of their makers. Early lithographed designs showed people and animals as silhouettes. Often a design featured simple lettering identifying "Seaside," "Atlantic City," "Coney Island," or even the well-known vacation message "A Present from [Jon]."

One particular beach pail motif was the Teddy Bear, popularized at the turn of the century. While some may know that this bear is named for Theodore "Teddy" Roosevelt, the story behind it is less well known. In November 1902 President Roosevelt was in Mississippi, trying to sort out a boundary problem between that state and neighboring Louisiana. During his trip he took time to go on a bear hunt. The hunting party itself did not go very well, but Roosevelt did come across a small bear cub. He decided to spare the life of the terrified animal, and the incident became the subject of full-page stories in newspapers throughout the country.

The cartoonist Clifford Berryman of the *Washington Star* made a cartoon depicting Roosevelt turning away from the cub, with a gun in one hand and raising his other to show that he would not shoot the young creature. The text below the cartoon read, "Drawing the Line in Mississippi." The cartoon was reprinted in newspapers around the country and started a nationwide love affair with Teddy Bears, named for the president who spared one.

The early sand pails depicting Teddy Bears are now of considerable value. In 1995, a sand pail depicting an early Teddy Bear on the beach sold at auction for $632.50 (today it would probably be worth over $1,000). The Teddy Bear was probably also the first popular character to appear on sand pails, although it would not be long before the radio and movies created new beloved heroes and cartoon creatures.

By the early decades of the twentieth century, it was practical to produce designs showing children or animals at play and include a background scene. These graphics were usually limited to the front and/or back of the pail. They were sometimes framed by a geometric or floral design. The First World War (1914–18) led to yet another burst of patriotic red, white, and blue. Until this time, German toys had been popular in the States, as they were beautifully designed and cheaper than American versions, but the war stopped their import. Once the European competition was removed, America was able to dominate the postwar toy industry by developing equipment for mass production and using the steady income from war work.

It is during this period that airplanes, dirigibles, bicycles, steamships, and motor cars also began to appear in the graphics on sand pails. The advent of the radio and movies in the 1930s created new heroes, characters, and cartoon creatures to be depicted on toys. Mickey and Minnie Mouse, Donald Duck, Snow White, and numerous other Disney characters all appeared on pails, spades, and sprinkling cans.

Between the Wars

The advances in toy production after the First World War were a reflection of the improvements in the U.S. economy. Prosperity and the emergence of the working middle class brought beach vacations within the grasp of millions of Americans. At this time, the bath houses still did good business (at 25 cents a dip), but the new rage was surf bathing—walking into the water as far as you dared, while holding onto a rope that led up to the beach. Tents and changing booths sprang up on the beaches for those willing to brave the waves. Even with extremely modest full-length bathing outfits that had been approved by both medical and religious authorities, ladies still had their own beaches.

In the 1920s the working man usually had weekends off, and after paying the bills he often had enough money left over for a week at the shore, or at

least a weekend excursion. In 1920 the New York Subway reached Coney Island, and in 1923 the beaches opened to the public. Almost overnight the resort became known as a "Nickel Empire," since nearly everything cost a nickel: getting there, Nathan's "red hot" dogs, Carnival side shows, shooting galleries, roller coaster rides, and Coca-Cola. On almost any Sunday in the mid-1920s a mass of one million city dwellers packed the beaches, all ready and willing to spend a pocketful of nickels. Nathan's alone had some fifty people serving thousands of frankfurters, hundreds of gallons of root beer, and truckloads of potato chips and knishes on a given day. Meanwhile the wealthier vacationers still patronized the more exclusive spots, like Luna Park and the Steeplechase.

Other resorts felt the same impact, as the day of the common man had arrived in many parts of the country. Asbury Park, which had rivaled Coney Island as a resort for the wealthy until it was devastated by the fire of 1917 and a storm in 1923, was rebuilt and became the place to go on the New Jersey Shore. In addition to swan boats and paddle boats on Wesley Lake, it offered pony rides and miniature golf on Ocean Avenue, pavilions for fresh- and saltwater bathing during the day, and dancing to the sounds of Big Bands at night.

Farther down the coast, Atlantic City grew and became known as "The Fountain-head of American Saltwater Bathing," with thirty thousand people in the sea at a time. Those who sought solitude were forced to travel to the distant, relatively unknown stretches of the Florida coast or the beaches of the Pacific. However, even in far-flung corners of the country, the railroad had changed everything. Railroad magnate Henry Flagler had agreed to extend his line to Miami in exchange for a large parcel of land there, and in 1896 the line opened. A year later Flagler opened the Royal Palm Hotel, built on his Miami site, for the jet-setters of the day. This was followed in 1924 by the Biltmore Hotel, which established the city as one of the world's great resorts—a reputation that lasted until the 1960s and was reborn in the 1990s, thanks to the revitalization and gentrification of South Beach, with its Art Deco architecture, exciting nightlife, and bustling restaurants.

The major change in the graphics found on pails in the 1930s was the evolution of the all-around design, where individual pictures were replaced with more complex images, sometimes with five-color printing. A single scene now wrapped around the pail, often featuring exotic animals seen in zoos or clowns and acrobats from the circus—then popular forms of entertainment. These themes continued to appear well into the 1950s. Beach pails in the 1930s also began being used as promotional items, primarily as novelty packaging for children's favorites like saltwater taffy and lollipops.

As the beach pail industry continued to grow, new giants of the industry emerged, such as the Ohio Art Company. This company was the brainchild of a former dentist and grocer, Henry S. Winzeler, who founded it in October 1908. It began with eight people who made metal picture frames on the second floor of the Ohio Band Hall in Archbold. By 1910 Winzeler was producing twenty thousand frames each day, for religious pictures and the "Cupid Awake" and "Cupid Asleep" lines that would be sold in Woolworth's for a few cents apiece. With the company's move to Bryan, Ohio, in early 1912 came a new production line of toy tin wagons and windmills. Ohio Art also introduced tin tea sets in 1918, followed by tops, drums, sand pails, shovels, and sprinkling cans in 1923. Later, they used Mickey and Minnie Mouse, Horace, Clarebell, and Pluto on their sand toys, as well as Pinocchio, Snow White and the Seven Dwarfs, and the Three Little Pigs, all under license from Walt Disney. Their toys are known for their exceptionally high-quality graphics, shown to great advantage on the sand pails, which offer a relatively large surface. In the 1930s and 1940s, Ohio Art utilized the talents of noted illustrators of children's books, including Fern Bisel Peat and Elaine Ends Hileman.

Peat created her classic versions of favorite nursery rhymes like "Humpty Dumpty," "Jack Be Nimble," and "Mary Had a Little Lamb." Other treasured designs by Peat are include the Gingham Dog and the Calico Cat, along with a beautiful selection of fairies, Dutch children, and frolicking kids. When toy production ceased during the Second World War, the Ohio Art Company, along with other American toy manufacturers, became involved with the war effort. Ohio Art subsequently received the highly prized Army-Navy Production Award for its services.

The Effects of World War II

On July 1, 1942, the government ordered the American Toy Industry to cease production of all toys made from metal or rubber for the duration of the war. This caused many small companies that lacked the resources to switch to weapons manufacturing to go out of business. Following the end of the war, raw materials became more readily available and the Ohio Art Company initiated toy production again, continuing its expansion and ultimately taking its rightful place among giants in the American lithographed tin toy industry. They bought Emenee Industries, makers of toy musical instruments, in 1969. The company is still active in Bryan, Ohio, best known today as the maker of the classic toy Etch-a-Sketch.

When toy production resumed after the war, the Sand Toy Company of Pittsburgh (later Wolverine) dominated the production of mechanical sand toys, derived from the ever-popular Sandy Andy. The market for beach pails, shovels, sifters, and molds was shared by the Ohio Art Company, J.

Chein & Company, and the U.S. Metal Toy Manufacturing Company. At first these companies focused on producing materials with the circus and farmyard scenes that had become popular in the 1930s, but as the effects of the war receded, designs were created that reflected the new heroes of radio and the silver screen. The "Wild West" was a particularly dominant theme on pails dating from these two decades, and nursery rhymes and letters of the alphabet continued to be popular.

The 1950s

The fifties are synonymous with the postwar baby boom, and a lot of sand pails were produced to meet the needs of those soon-to-be toddlers. This was the dawn of the Atomic Age, when the U.S. Navy launched the first nuclear-powered submarine. Since the concept of space travel also was becoming popular (there was even a rise in the number of UFO sightings), spacemen and alien themes captured the public's imagination and dominated many movie and radio programs.

In October 1957, fantasy turned into reality, as the U.S.S.R.'s Sputnik marked the arrival of the Space Age. The race to the moon had begun. A huge inter-

est was emerging in science and technology as well, and all of this was reflected in the emergence of space toys. Flying saucers, intergalactic battles, robots, and ray guns captivated youngsters aspiring to become fearless space heroes. Sand pails sporting cowboys and Indians were replaced by those featuring astronauts and aliens. Snoopy and Charlie Brown, who had made their debut in the Peanuts comic strip in 1950, would soon find their way onto sand pails as well.

Fifties icons had tremendous impact on consumer life in America. Since more than two-thirds of American families owned a television set by the mid-1950s, characters that were easily recognized were successfully marketed. It was the decade of Marilyn Monroe, Marlon Brando, Steve McQueen, and Elvis Presley; Cinemascope was introduced to the cinema screens, Fender launched their Stratocaster electric guitar, and Ian Fleming published the first James Bond novel. Disneyland opened in California and the first shopping mall opened in Detroit. As the Korean War ended, there was more leisure time, and more people took short breaks and holidays, even coming back to the beach.

The pails produced in this period featured graphics bursting with vitality and colors with a distinctive brightness, richness, and clarity. The highest quality pails of the period arguably came from a small family business based in the Bayridge section of Brooklyn. T. Cohn and Superior Toys made beautifully lithographed pails along with candy pails, sprinkling cans, and other tin toys. As children, Mr. Cohn's daughters had helped with the company designs. Cohn's pails are noteworthy for their exceptional quality, not only in manufacture but also in the wonderful graphics and depth of colors—especially reds, oranges, and greens. Cohn's scenes of children and animals at play, which are probably the most popular and enduring themes for beach pails, are as good as the best that Ohio Art or J. Chein could produce with much larger budgets.

As was the case with many pail makers, T. Cohn's insistence on high-quality graphics meant the company could not devote the resources to keeping up with the number of new characters that were emerging on television. The "Wild West"

was a dominant theme of the '40s and '50s, yet pails with a Western motif incorporated only generic cowboy characters instead of Gene Autry, The Lone Ranger, Hop-Along Cassidy, and Roy Rogers, who did appear with great popularity on lunch boxes, boards games, and other toys. Ironically, the toy makers' own high standards would eventually contribute to their demise.

The Sun Sets on Tin: Plastics

When it was first introduced, plastic was promoted as "the material of the future." Industries began to use plastic to manufacture items they had made for decades out of more conventional materials. Suddenly on the market were designer Russell Wright's Melamine tableware, Tupperware containers for food storage, and Formica countertops, tables, and dinette sets—all promoted as a housewife's dream. From a marketing standpoint the miracle of plastic was that it could be made to look like much more valuable and refined materials, like marble speckled with gold. This lent an air of luxuriousness to every middle-class home—at an affordable price.

Plastics were used to make items that appeared in every room. In children's rooms, toy boxes that were once filled with metal soldiers and farm animals now contained molded plastic forms. Many traditional dolls fashioned from papier-mâché or exquisite porcelain were discarded in favor of easy-to-clean and hard-to-break plastic versions. It was only a matter of time before the decorated tin sand pail would meet the same fate.

Graphics on beach toys became much more stylized in the 1960s. "Flower Power" influenced many designs, but in large part the vivid colors and detailed graphics disappeared. Sand pails once again were used for promotional advertising, which often covered the graphics altogether with a paper label. The Japanese now dominated much of the tin toy industry. Their factories were newer and labor was cheaper, so they were able to produce toys, novelties, and trinkets far cheaper than could be done in America.

With the 1970s came an even more widespread use of plastics. This was the beginning of the end for the beautifully lithographed sand pails. Some toy companies held out for a while, but the graphics became less detailed. Plastic was so influential it caused the tin sand toy virtually to disappear, and along with it, a portion of the American toy industry. With the switch from tin to plastic, beach pails went from magical to practical. The vivid scenes that wrapped the pails were gone, as were the multicolored graphics. Selections available to a child in a store went from cowboys, astronauts, Cinderella, or Snow White to red, yellow, or blue.

Tin Men: Profiles of Two Twentieth-Century Toy Magnates

Louis Marx

Of all the "tin men" in the industry, the most famous is probably Louis Marx. He spent his entire working life in the industry. Born in Brooklyn in 1896, Marx started out as an office boy for Ferdinand Strauss, "The Toy King," and by age twenty he became a director at Strauss' company. Marx left the Strauss Company to form the Marx Toy Company in 1919. He was soon joined by his brother David. Their company maxims were, "Quality is not negotiable," "Give the customer more toy for less money," and "Quality at the lowest price." Initially the brothers designed the toys and then subcontracted out the manufacturing, but by 1921 they themselves were able to make the toys they designed. The company grew rapidly and later expanded to Canada and Great Britain, using factories in Australia, Brazil, France, Germany, Japan, Mexico, and South Africa.

A 1928 wholesaler's catalog features two sand toys with the Marx logo: a Ferris wheel and windmill, and both are similar to the early mechanical sand toys. Sand pails and shovels that do not have a producer's label are also shown, and given Marx's entrepreneurial skills, these, too, probably stemmed from his empire.

Marx's tin toys sold extremely well and he was a millionaire by the time he was thirty. The huge showrooms were a virtual toy fair in themselves. Marx did not spend much on advertising campaigns or a large sales force. He became very successful by concentrating his marketing efforts on selling in vast quantities to chain stores, department stores, and mail order houses such as Sears. The buyers came to Louis Marx and ninety percent of the toys were sold in his New York showrooms, located at 200 Fifth Avenue. He had a reputation as a shrewd business-man who produced millions of toys at the lowest prices, kept manufacturing costs down, and was always in search of cheaper labor or sources of raw materials. In wartime he used tin cans and scrap tin to produce his toys, and evidence of this can still be found in some of them. A brilliant capitalist, Marx often copied and then undersold toys made by other companies, and by the 1950s he could claim to be the largest toy manufacturer in the world.

In 1972, when Marx was in his seventies, he sold his worldwide company to the Quaker Oats conglomerate. After four years, they sold the toy division to Europe's largest toy manufacturer, Dunbee-Combex. By then, plastics had revolutionized the industry and the tin toy era was over. The new owners declared bankruptcy in 1980. Marx himself died just two years later.

Julius Chein

In 1903, Julius Chein, an immigrant from Russia, started a tin toy company in a loft on West Broadway in Manhattan. Early prosperity was largely due to a contract to produce tin watches and the small "clicking cricket" toys that were inserted in boxes of a new confection called "Cracker Jack." Chein was prolific in lithographed and sheet metal toy production and specialized in mechanical toys, banks, drums, tea sets, tops, and pails. Most of his company's production was for F. W. Woolworth's.

In the 1920s the Chein Manufacturing Company led the way in depicting comic characters like Popeye and Krazy Cat (also known as Felix). This was followed in the 1930s by Mickey and Minnie Mouse who, along with Raggedy Ann and Andy, kept the company profitable until the '60s, when the Peanuts comic strip characters took over. Chein was also one of the few manufacturers ever to produce square sand pails, which today fetch a price with collectors.

The power of character images continued even after the company ceased making toys and began to manufacture housewares under the name Atlantic Cheinco. Machines that had been used to make beach pails began to produce illustrated paint buckets and wastebaskets. An early wastebasket lithograph design of a sailing boat was followed by Coca-Cola, "Happy Face," and Star Wars motifs. These proved to be very successful, culminating in 1989 with the Teenage Mutant Ninja Turtles wastebasket, which became one of the most profitable items in Chein's history with more than two million dollars in sales.

These sand pails are unmarked, but their designs
are reminiscent of those of the Ohio Art Co.

TO GOLD, the smell of the sea at Sheepshead Bay was a powerful call to clams on the half shell, shrimp, lobster, or broiled flounder or bass.

from *Good as Gold* by Joseph Heller (1923–1999)
American author

IT was easy to see Mark again because he was always on the beach. He was always in the same place, always alone. Each time I saw him lying on a white towel in the sun, jeans and sweat shirt neatly folded by his side, his tan was deeper. Often he seemed to be asleep. Sometimes he propped himself up on one elbow and lazily watched people strolling along the shore.

Gavin Lamber
20th Century American writer

The construction of this unmarked pail is similar to many originating in Europe.
For prime examples of other European pails, see page 99.

This classic pail depicts the traditional children's rhyme, "Winken, Blinken, and Nod."

I do Like to be Beside the Seaside

Song title by John A. Glover-Kind (19th Century)
American songwriter

It is perhaps a more fortunate destiny

to have a taste for collecting

shells than to be born a millionaire.

Robert Louis Stevenson (1850–1894)
Scottish novelist, poet, and essayist

T. Bros. produced several designs with patriotic themes
to pay homage to our boys "over there."

A simple but magnificent graphic full of adventure, discovery, and wonder by the Metal Package Corp.

One cannot collect

all the beautiful shells on the beach.

One can collect only a few,

and they are more beautiful if they are few.

from *Gift From The Sea* by Anne Morrow Lindbergh (1906–2001)
American writer and pilot

The Walrus
and the Carpenter

Were walking close at hand;

They wept like anything to see

Such quantities of sand:

'If this were only cleaned away,'

They said,
'It would be grand!'

from *Through the Looking Glass* by Lewis Carroll (1832–1898)
English author

Ohio Art is best known for their depictions of children,
but this wonderful pail shows a delightful animal scene.

This trio of turn-of-the-century pails were imported
from either Germany or France.

The moonlight touched

the tips of the waves with silver,

and, as I had done many

times alone, I walked to the shore . . .

and entered the water.

from *Ahab's Wife* by Sena Jeter Naslund
American author

THE people walked in little groups toward the beach. They talked and laughed; some of them sang. . . . Most of them walked into the water as though into a natural element. The sea was quiet now, and swelled lazily in broad billows that melted into another and did not break except upon the beach in little foamy crests that coiled back like slow, white serpents.

From *The Awakening* by Kate Chopin (1851–1904)
American author

These children don't seem to be having much fun in their formal clothes.
AMSCO of New Jersey was one of the early pailmakers who went out of business quickly.

This particular toy windmill is marked E. Rosen, but others identical in design have been marked T. Cohn. An explanation of the discrepancy might be explained if T. Cohn made it for E. Rosen. The colors, the farmer, and the cart are typical of T. Cohn designs.

I've never seen the point of the sea, except where it meets the land.

The shore has a point. The sea has none.

Alan Bennett
English writer and actor

It is the drawback of all seaside places that half the landscape is unavailable for purposes of human locomotion, being covered by useless water.

from *Alone* by Norman Douglas (1868–1952)
British novelist

Two French pails.

Beach Pails Today

Collecting Pails

One way to relive the memories inspired by pails of the past is to start your own collection of beach pails. Interestingly, sand pails have entranced a whole new generation of collectors. They even have been embraced by people who had never previously given the subject of collecting antiques a thought. Why? Because they are colorful, decorative, and nostalgic, and they can be displayed to make lovely focal points in a room.

Pails are extremely popular with the thirties-something crowd who can just about remember the last of the decorated tin pails and shovels, sifters, and sprinkling cans. Often they use their prized collection to decorate a high shelf in the baby's nursery and, who knows, by the time baby is ready to go off to college, the pail collection might go a long way to paying for the cost of school.

Others who are hot on the trail of pails are looking to decorate their seaside cottage or summer home. Pails give these quiet and peaceful havens a wonderful nostalgic air and evoke fond memories of childhood summers spent at the beach.

We have a theory that people who collect sand pails had a happy childhood. This may or may not be true but few collectibles seem to evoke such happy memories as the simple sand pail. They are a fun collectible, but because they have become so popular, values have risen, and putting together a collection can require a real investment.

Placing a Value on Nostalgia

For many years sand pails had been neglected by serious lithographed tin toy collectors who opted for larger, more opulent toys than the then-regarded lowly-sand pail. These collectors seemed to forget that most of the toy companies turning out "serious" tin toys were also manufacturing countless numbers of sand toys, using the same vibrant colors in their lithography, and the same designers, artists, and famous children's book illustrators for their artwork. These collectors also seemed to forget that many of the sand toys were neglected at the end of the summer season and were left to rust away, making those that remained in good shape relatively rare. Now, when prime examples of beach pails are found, a long forgotten design is unearthed, or a pail signed by a noted illustrator is discovered, that pail has become just as "serious" as the other toys of yesteryear.

Just a few years ago it was possible to visit almost any flea market and buy a pail for $20. Today, unless you are very lucky, or the pail is in very bad condition, it's a different story. Prices range from $50 to a few thousand dollars, so it's worth knowing a few things about valuation.

Condition determines just about everything to do with cost. A pail may be worth $500 or $5 depending on condition. Rust, dents, missing parts and major scratches have a serious impact on value.

Popularity also affects price. If you collect particular themes, such as fashions, transport, space travel, occupations, Nursery Rhymes, circus, farmyard, domestic or wild animals, or simply scenes of children playing, then there are many affordable examples to provide a colorful addition to your collection. However, for well-preserved Victorian, Edwardian, early Patriotic designs, dirigibles, airplanes, resorts (like Coney Island and Atlantic City), early Teddy Bears, or anything Disney, be prepared to pay a premium.

The abrasive and corrosive combination of saltwater and sand has made collecting any of these early sand toys a challenge, but the hunt for specimens in good condition is well worth the effort. Most of the "mint" or "near mint" examples available today were probably warehouse or shop stock that never reached a child's hands. These pristine pails are the most valuable, although they lack the charm of slight fading, minor scratches, and even small dents on toys that were used and loved. However, any pail that shows significant wear and tear is of little value and is not likely to appreciate significantly.

Identifying Yesterday's Pails

As hard as it is to believe today, toy makers in the late nineteenth century generally did not mark their products with a company imprint, which means it is virtually impossible to trace a pail to an individual manufacturer. It is also difficult to distinguish American pails of the period from those that were imported from Europe. Unfortunately, relatively few of these very early American pails have survived, but it is still possible, with a little patience, to put together a collection of these Victorian toys that traces their early development.

From the 1920s onwards, pail manufacturers did begin to identify their wares by incorporating trademarks in their graphics. Shopkeepers used inked rubber stamps or paper labels to mark the retail price, which can sometimes still be found on the bottom of a pail. These are details that collectors use to estimate the age of individual toys.

Beach Pails Today

Next time you wander along the beach on a glorious summer's day, take a look at the children playing in the sand, building their sand castles, or running to the water's edge to fill their pails with sea water. They may not look like the tin pails you remember, but the joy they bring to the children ankle-deep in sand is the same.

What is more, the tin beach pail is making a comeback! A few enterprising companies have recently started to manufacture tin sand pails with colorful graphics that have a certain air of nostalgia about them. The scenes on the pails cannot match the memories of childhood past, but they do provide a new generation of children, parents, and grandparents with the simple pleasure of a colorful toy that turns the imagination to flights of fancy and brings smiles to eager young faces.

You listen to the quiet song of waves and to the group of ducks in the reeds near the rocky islet, and the idyll is so perfect, that no art can create anything more perfect. . . .

Eino Kaila (1890–1958)
Finnish philosopher

Three small embossed pails from Germany, circa late 1800s.

These designs by J. Chein were used on pails of at least three different sizes.
Chein also often used the same artwork on different items.

Always the edge of the sea

remains an elusive and indefinable boundary.

The shore has a dual nature, changing

with the swing of the tides, belonging now

to the land, now to the sea.

from *The Edge of the Sea* by Rachel Carson (1907–1964)
American writer and environmentalist

I knew in my house and garden by the sea under the sun, there is pure timelessness.

from *Outer Banks* by Anne Rivers Siddons
American author

Little is known about YLES, the manufacturer of these charming pails.

Mechanical sand toy, maker unknown. Winding a handle
makes the buckets carry sand up to the funnel that dumps into a wagon, which,
when full, travels down the ramp and refills the bin at the bottom.

My soul is full of longing

For the secret of the Sea,

And the heart of the great ocean

Sends a thrilling pulse
through me.

from "The Secret of the Sea"
by Henry Wadsworth Longfellow (1807–1882)
American poet

The sea pronounces something, over and over,

in a hoarse whisper; I cannot quite make it out.

from *Teaching a Stone to Talk* by Annie Dillard
American writer and poet

A trio of pails from the early 1900s. The two with stars are almost certainly by T. Bros.
For other examples of patriotic pails, see page 125.

Early American pails decorated to celebrate the summer. The pail on the left is by T. Bros. and the one below is a nice example of the work of Amsco.

The voice of the sea speaks to the soul.

The touch of the sea is sensuous,

enfolding the body in its soft, close embrace.

from *The Awakening* by Kate Chopin (1851–1904)
American author

Buoyed by water,

he can fly in any direction—

up, down, sideways—by merely

flipping his hand.

Under water, man becomes

an archangel.

Jacques-Yves Cousteau (1910–1997)
French oceanographer and explorer

This is almost certainly of European origin, probably from Spain or Italy.
The interior decoration makes this pail a special treat.

Unusual shapes are always fun. The square pail comes from England and was made by Happynak.
The boat was made by the American Banner Plastics Corporation.

. . . I stepped into the ocean, into real water, for the first time in my life. I had absolutely no fear, and though I couldn't swim yet, I could almost immediately ride the waves. Somehow, I sensed, the water was my natural element. This is where I belonged. It was only a matter of days before I learned to swim . . .

Esther Williams
American swimmer

TO ME, the sea is like a child that I've known for a long time. It sounds crazy, I know, but when I swim in the sea I talk to it. I never feel alone when I'm out there.

Gertrude Ederle
American swimmer, first woman to successfully
swim the English channel

Another view of the T. Cohn pail shown on page 14.

This typical T. Bros design is simple and commercial but lacks a sense of fun.
However, it is a great find for Atlantic City buffs.

The sea! The sea! The open sea!

The blue, the fresh, the ever free!

from "The Sea" by Barry Cornwall (1787–1874)
English poet

THE SEA KNOWS ALL THINGS, for at night when the winds are asleep the stars confide to him their secrets. In his breast are stored away all the elements that go to make up the round world. Beneath his depths lie buried the sunken kingdoms of fable and legend, whose monarchs have long been lost in oblivion. . . . It is not to be wondered that men have worshiped the ocean, for in his depths they have seen mirrored the image of Eternity—of Infinity.

from "The Sea" by Elbert Hubbard (1856–1915)
American editor, publisher, and author

These twentieth century pails depict patriotism and the summertime,
two great themes of celebration. On the left, a very cute marching children scene
by an unknown artist; the American eagle pail in the center was manufactured
by Otcco Art; and on the right, a playful T. Bros design

Photo Credits

Beach pails and sand toys courtesy of:

Joanne and Donald Davidow: 2, 13, 22 left, 25, 33, 34, 37, 38, 45, 52 right, 55, 56, 60, 87, 92, 95, 99 left, 105, 106 right, 109, 114 left and top, 125, 126.

Myra and Byron Prusky: 11, 14, 18, 21 (bottom), 29, 91, 106 left, 117, 121, 128.

Toby and Stephen Schachman: 1, 7, 8 right, left, and bottom, 17, 21 top, 22 right, 30, 42, 46, 51, 52 left, 63, 64, 67, 76, 80, 83, 84, 88, 99 right, 113, 114 bottom, 118 right, 122.

I do Like to be Beside the Seaside

Song title by John A. Glover-Kind (19th Century)
American songwriter

The sea pronounces something, over and over,
in a hoarse whisper; I cannot quite make it out.

from Teaching a Stone to Talk by Annie Dillard
American writer and poet

Dandelion wine.

The words were summer on the tongue.

Ray Bradbury
American author

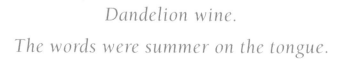